NUCLEAR
WEAPONS

NUCLEAR WEAPONS

BY SUSAN M. FREESE

Content Consultant
Michael Andregg, PhD
adjunct instructor, justice and peace studies
University of St. Thomas

ABDO
Publishing Company

CREDITS

Published by ABDO Publishing Company, 8000 West 78th Street, Edina, Minnesota 55439. Copyright © 2012 by Abdo Consulting Group, Inc. International copyrights reserved in all countries. No part of this book may be reproduced in any form without written permission from the publisher. The Essential Library™ is a trademark and logo of ABDO Publishing Company.

Printed in the United States of America, North Mankato, Minnesota
062011
092011

 THIS BOOK CONTAINS AT LEAST 10% RECYCLED MATERIALS.

Editor: Karen Latchana Kenney
Copy Editor: Jennifer Joline Anderson
Design and Production: Marie Tupy

Library of Congress Cataloging-in-Publication Data
Freese, Susan M., 1958-
  Nuclear weapons / by Susan M. Freese.
     p. cm. -- (Essential issues)
  Includes bibliographical references and index.
  ISBN 978-1-61783-137-9
  1. Nuclear weapons--Juvenile literature. 2. Nuclear warfare--Juvenile literature. I. Title.
  U264.F729 2011
  355.02'17--dc22

                                   2011009734

TABLE OF CONTENTS

*Smoke billowed from Yeonpyeong, South Korea,
after it was attacked on November 23, 2010.*

GLOBAL TENSIONS
IN THE NUCLEAR AGE

On November 23, 2010, the military of North Korea fired dozens of artillery shells at Yeonpyeong, a small island off South Korea. The attack, which lasted approximately 90 minutes, killed two South Korean soldiers and injured 20 others.

The attack on Yeonpyeong was widely reported by the US media, but the news did not seem especially important to most Americans. What most Americans did not realize, however, was that the conflict in Korea had the potential to spark a nuclear war.

CONFLICT ON THE KOREAN PENINSULA

The island of Yeonpyeong is located in the Yellow Sea, near the border of North Korea and South Korea. That border has been an ongoing source of conflict between the two nations since 1953. That year marked the end of the Korean War (1950–1953), when a cease-fire was called after three years of fighting between North Korea and South Korea and their allies.

The November 23, 2010, shelling was not the first time the North had attacked the South. Just eight months earlier, in March 2010, North Korea sank a South Korean naval vessel, killing 46 crew members. However, the attack on Yeonpyeong was the first time the North had targeted a location where the residents included South Korean civilians.

South Korea's strongest ally, the United States, immediately condemned the attack. President Barack Obama called it outrageous. Other world leaders joined the criticism of North Korea and called the attack "unprovoked."[1] North Korean leaders responded by stating that they had attacked in defense of their nation. They claimed that South Korea had been conducting military drills in the area and refused to stop despite having been warned to do so.

There were several reasons why world leaders were troubled by the timing of North Korea's show of military force. A group of US nuclear weapons experts had recently concluded, after

---

The Korean War

The Korean War was a conflict between North and South Korea that lasted from 1950 to 1953. The war had its roots in a tumultuous history. From 1910 to 1945, Japan had ruled the entire country of Korea. Following Japan's surrender at the end of World War II, Korea was divided in half and controlled by other nations. The northern half was controlled by the Soviet Union and the southern half was controlled by the United States.

Conflict soon developed between the North and the South. In 1948, plans to hold elections and establish a unified Korean government fell through, and North Korea established its own Communist government. While negotiations about reunifying the two Koreas continued, small battles and raids occurred along the border that divided them. Finally, on June 25, 1950, the conflict turned into all-out warfare, with the North invading the South.

The United Nations (UN) came to the assistance of South Korea, sending troops from the United States, the United Kingdom, Canada, and other UN member countries. China and the Soviet Union both came to the aid of North Korea. The Korean War ended with a cease-fire agreement in 1953. The original border dividing North Korea and South Korea was maintained, but it remained a source of conflict into 2011.

looking at surveillance photographs taken by military satellites, that the North Koreans had built a facility for enriching uranium. Enriched uranium can be used to fuel nuclear power plants, but it is also used in nuclear weapons. A US nuclear scientist confirmed the finding after touring the North Korean facility during a private visit in early November 2010. He later stated that he had been surprised by how advanced the facility was.

Especially troublesome to world leaders was the fact that this state-of-the-art facility had been built quite recently. It had not existed in April 2009, the last time North Korea had allowed nuclear inspectors in the country. The speed with which the facility had been built, along with its advanced capability, suggested that North Korea had had technological and financial help from another country.

World leaders were also troubled by North Korea's announcement

Recent History of North and South Korea

2000: Leaders from the two nations meet to establish formal communication.

2002: North and South Korean patrol boats fire on one another near the disputed border in the Yellow Sea.

2003: North Korea withdraws from the Nuclear Nonproliferation Treaty (NPT).

2006: North Korea announces it has successfully tested a nuclear weapon.

2007: Leaders from the two nations sign a permanent peace treaty.

2009: The navies of North and South Korea clash again in the Yellow Sea.

2010: A South Korean warship is split in two by a torpedo from a submarine. North Korea denies involvement, but evidence supports their involvement.

Kim Jong Un will take control of North Korea after his father dies.

about a transition of leadership, which came just six weeks after the attack on Yeonpyeong. The country's ruler, Kim Jong Il, announced that when he left office he would be replaced by his youngest son, Kim Jong Un. Kim Jong Un, believed to be only 27 or 28 years old, was not expected to take over until after his father's death. Even so, his aging father's poor health, combined with his own lack of leadership experience, caused concern among world leaders. They worried that the young Kim might try to prove himself by making a reckless military move—perhaps one involving the use of a nuclear weapon.

DEVELOPMENT OF A NUCLEAR WORLD

The world has lived with the threat of nuclear war since 1945, when the United States dropped two atomic bombs on Japan to end World War II (1939– 1945). The bombings of the cities of Hiroshima and Nagasaki on August 6 and August 9, respectively, killed approximately 200,000 people immediately and 340,000 more within five years. Countless more people suffered for the rest of their lives from cancer and other long-term effects of radiation poisoning, a lingering effect of the bombings.

To date, the US bombings of Japan mark the only uses of nuclear weapons against humans in history. However, since World War II, the development of nuclear weapons has continued at an alarming pace. By 2010, nine countries were known to have nuclear weapons capabilities.

From the late 1940s to the early 1990s, the threat of nuclear war came primarily from the world's two superpowers: the United States and the Soviet Union. After World War II, both nations focused intently on developing new types of nuclear weapons and new ways of delivering them across great distances. The two superpowers built up huge arsenals, so that by 1985, they possessed enough nuclear weapons to destroy the entire world many times over.

The superpowers' ability to destroy one another—along with the rest of the world—was called mutual assured destruction (MAD). In effect, the United States and the Soviet Union were at a standoff. They were enemies, but neither dared to take military action, knowing that nuclear war could destroy them both. The 45-year period of deterrence between the world's two superpowers was known as the Cold War (1945–1991). It ended in 1991 with the collapse of the Soviet Union.

The end of the Cold War did not mean the end of the nuclear threat, however. Several other countries had already begun developing nuclear weapons. By the mid-1960s, the United Kingdom, France, and China all had nuclear weapons.

Recognizing the increased potential for nuclear war, world leaders began negotiating weapons

The Start of the Cold War

The Korean War was the first conflict in the period known as the Cold War. In that conflict, the United States and the Soviet Union—who were allies against Japan and Germany in World War II—found themselves fighting one another in defense of their new territories, democratic South Korea and Communist North Korea, respectively. For many Americans, the Korean War demonstrated the threat of Soviet Communist influence. Recognizing this threat helped the United States justify the huge military build-up that would follow—particularly, the development of nuclear weapons.

control. A series of treaties were put in place to control the testing and deployment of nuclear weapons. One treaty in particular—the Nuclear Nonproliferation Treaty (NPT) of 1968—was aimed at preventing more countries from developing nuclear weapons. Even with the NPT in place, several more countries proceeded with nuclear weapons programs.

During the 1980s and 1990s, India, Israel, South Africa, and Pakistan were all revealed to have nuclear arsenals. India, Pakistan, and Israel refused to sign the NPT. North Korea signed the treaty but later withdrew from it and has refused to allow inspection of its nuclear facilities. The continuing development of nuclear weapons is alarming for many reasons. The fact that more countries have these weapons increases the likelihood of a nuclear war or accidents involving nuclear weapons. Also of concern to the countries of the NPT is the fact that some countries gaining nuclear capabilities, including India, North Korea, and Pakistan, are considered politically unstable or undeveloped. Undeveloped countries often have politically corrupt regimes. Terrorist groups may also have influence with their government policies or actions.

An additional threat comes from the possibility that nuclear weapons traffickers will provide an unstable nation or terrorist group with the materials or technology needed to build a nuclear weapon. In 2004, the government of Pakistan admitted that the engineer who led its nuclear weapons program, A. Q. Khan, had been conducting a so-called rogue operation. Khan had likely provided assistance with weapons development to North Korea, Iran, and Libya, but the full extent of his operation could not be confirmed.

A US weapons expert verified that the Pakistani engineer had released a detailed design for a small but powerful nuclear weapon—one that could be launched from a vehicle using a far-ranging missile. The weapon blueprints could easily have been shared with other nations such as Iran and Syria, or with terrorist groups. After examining the design, the expert asked the question that was likely on the minds of people all over the world: "Who else had it?"[2]

Nuclear Weapons Tests

Between 1945 and 2008, an estimated 2,000 tests of nuclear weapons were conducted worldwide—mostly before 1991 by the United States and the Soviet Union. The United States conducted approximately 900 tests at its primary facility, the Nevada Test Site. Additional tests were conducted at sites across the Soviet Union by the Soviets and in the South Pacific by the United States.

The founder of Pakistan's nuclear program, Khan,
leaked nuclear secrets to other countries.

*Danish physicist Niels Bohr, left, studied electrons,
which paved the way toward nuclear weapons development.*

BUILDING THE BOMB

*I*n the late 1800s and early 1900s, atomic research laid the groundwork for the development of nuclear weapons. In 1897, English physicist Joseph John Thomson discovered the electron, one of several kinds of particles inside an atom. In 1911, New Zealand physicist Ernest Rutherford discovered the nucleus, which is the dense core of the atom. Two years later, in 1913, Danish physicist Niels Bohr extended Rutherford's work to explain how electrons give off energy.

SPLITTING THE ATOM

In the coming years, atomic research focused on splitting the atom. In 1933, Hungarian physicist Leo Szilard theorized that splitting a very large single atom might cause other atoms to split in a nuclear chain reaction. He suggested that as an atom split, it would release energy. The resulting total release of energy could then cause an explosion. In 1938, German scientist Otto Hahn and his colleagues announced they had successfully bombarded uranium, a chemical element, with neutrons, which produced peculiar changes to the uranium.

A year later, in 1939, Austrian physicists Lise Meitner and Otto Frisch reviewed Hahn's findings and proved that the uranium atoms had actually been split. Even more remarkable, the splitting process had created more energy than it had used. Meitner and Frisch concluded that it was possible to split an atom in a process called fission.

The German Scientists

In 1933—just 15 years after the end of World War I (1914–1918)—the world was once again on the path to global conflict. Adolf Hitler and his Nazi Party came to power in Germany. The Nazis put in place strict, discriminatory laws that took away the rights of Jews and people of other ethnic and religious groups. Many German scientists were fired from their positions as researchers and professors by laws that prohibited Jews from holding positions of authority.

One of those individuals was Albert Einstein— perhaps the world's best-

Atoms, Elements, and Radioactivity

An atom is made up of three kinds of particles: protons, neutrons, and electrons. Protons and neutrons are grouped together tightly in the center of the atom. Together, they form the nucleus. The electrons float in the space outside the nucleus of the atom.

The atoms of different elements have different numbers of protons, neutrons, and electrons. An atom of hydrogen, for instance, has one proton and one electron but no neutrons. An atom of uranium, on the other hand, has 92 protons, 146 neutrons, and 92 electrons. Elements with large numbers of particles, which are referred to as "heavy," are highly radioactive.

In early research on atoms, scientists discovered that some elements are made up of atoms that are naturally unstable. These atoms are constantly changing and sending out streams of particles in a process called radioactivity. Scientists proved that when directed at an atom, these flying particles could be used like tiny missiles to split the atom. Conducting further research, scientists found ways of using radioactive particles to bombard atoms, forcing them to split.

known scientist at the time. As the result of his groundbreaking research, Einstein had won the Nobel Prize in Physics in 1921. In 1933, alarmed by the developments in Nazi Germany, Einstein left his homeland and relocated to the United States. Like Einstein, approximately 400 German scientists left their homeland in the 1930s. And as World War II threatened to break out across Europe, other scientists fled their homelands and many went to the United States.

The German physicists who relocated to the United States knew their colleagues at home were continuing to study atomic fission. Afraid that Hitler and the Nazis would produce an atomic bomb, Leo Szilard and several other scientists wanted to warn US President Franklin D. Roosevelt of this possibility.

In July 1939, Szilard convinced Einstein to contact Roosevelt on behalf of the scientists. On August 2, 1939, Einstein sent a letter to the president outlining atomic research that had been conducted in Germany and explaining that it could be used to produce "extremely powerful bombs."[1] Einstein's letter also encouraged Roosevelt to set up a US research team to coordinate and speed up the work currently being conducted at separate universities across the country.

After receiving the letter in October, Roosevelt responded by setting up a committee to promote research into creating an atomic bomb. And in just over a year, work on building that bomb was underway.

THE MANHATTAN PROJECT

The project to build an atomic bomb was launched in December 1941. It was assigned the code name the Manhattan Project. The military officer in charge of the project was Brigadier General Leslie R. Groves, and the scientific director was physicist J. Robert Oppenheimer. Given an unlimited budget by the president, the project was expected to produce results quickly.

The primary research facility for the Manhattan Project was at Los Alamos, an isolated area of New Mexico. Approximately 6,000 people came to work and live there—most of them scientists and technicians and their families. Across the country, another 200,000 Americans worked

"From the day I was assigned to the Project there was never any doubt [that] my mission . . . was to get this thing done and used as quickly as possible, and every effort was bent toward that assignment."[2]
—*General Leslie R. Groves, military director of the Manhattan Project*

on the Manhattan Project in various engineering and industrial positions. Very few of these individuals knew the real nature of their work. Likewise, only a few US military and political leaders knew about the Manhattan Project. Even the ultimate cost of the project, estimated at $2 billion, was kept from the US Congress.

In the summer of 1944, General Groves told President Roosevelt that several atomic bombs would be ready for use the following year—news the president was eager to hear. But Roosevelt would not live to see the Manhattan Project completed. He died on April 12, 1945. When Vice President Harry S. Truman became president, he was immediately briefed about the project. Not even he had known anything about it before becoming president.

Making Key Decisions

With the surrender of Germany in May 1945, Japan remained the only possible target for the United States' use of an atomic bomb. A committee called the Interim Committee was set up to make key decisions about using the bomb and to advise President Truman. The committee had to decide whether to first bomb a city or a deserted place in Japan and whether to warn the Japanese of the upcoming attack. The committee's unanimous recommendation was to drop the bomb on a city without warning. The committee also had to determine which specific Japanese cities to bomb. They wanted to select a site that would demonstrate the bomb's full destructive force. After considering many sites, they selected Hiroshima as the first target and Nagasaki as the second.

In July 1945, a meeting was held between President Truman and other Allied leaders, Prime Minister Winston Churchill of Great Britain and Premier Joseph Stalin of the Soviet Union. The purpose of this meeting, called the Potsdam Conference, was to discuss how best to end the war with Japan and to make plans for the future political leadership of Europe. The Allies decided to issue a formal statement to Japan, demanding the nation's surrender.

Similar discussions were being held in Japan. Some of the nation's

Selecting Hiroshima and Nagasaki

The city of Hiroshima, with its population of 255,000, was selected as the ideal target because it had a seaport and a sizable army base. In addition, it had suffered little damage thus far in the war and was of the right geographic size to demonstrate the tremendous power of the bomb. Hiroshima was also located on a flat piece of land, which would further demonstrate the bomb's power.

The second target, Nagasaki, had a population of 195,000. It was a major industrial center in Japan, but in terms of geography, it was less desirable. This city was surrounded by hills, which would limit the impact of the explosion.

A "Fat Man" type of nuclear bomb was built during the Manhattan Project.

leaders believed the situation was hopeless and that they should negotiate an immediate end to the war. Others were determined to fight to the finish, at all costs.

LITTLE BOY AND FAT MAN

Also in the summer of 1945, the Manhattan Project team built two types of atomic bombs. One bomb, nicknamed "Little Boy," was made using uranium. The team was so certain this technology would work that they did not even test the bomb before its use. The second bomb was nicknamed

"Fat Man." It was made using plutonium, a rare radioactive element. The team was less certain this device would work, so they scheduled a test.

The Trinity Test was conducted just before sunrise on July 16, 1945, in the New Mexico desert. The scientists and technicians who observed the test were reported to have mixed feelings about it. According to Oppenheimer, the mood following the test was "extremely solemn."[3]

The materials for the two bombs were shipped to Tinian Island, in the South Pacific, in the summer of 1945. Truman formally authorized the use of atomic bombs against Japan on July 25, 1945. The next day, the Allies issued the Potsdam Declaration, which asked the Japanese government to surrender or face "prompt and utter destruction."[4] Two days later, on July 28, the Japanese prime minister refused the Allies' request. With this refusal, the fate of Hiroshima was sealed. It would be the site of the world's first atomic bombing.

Conflict Over Japan Bomb Warning

US Navy Admiral Lewis Strauss recommended dropping the atomic bomb on a large forest just outside Tokyo to issue a warning to the Japanese government. Oppenheimer disagreed, arguing that this sort of demonstration would not likely bring about surrender. Secretary of State James Byrnes disagreed with the idea of warning the Japanese as to when and where the bombing would occur.

The Trinity Test proved the destructive power of the "Fat Man" bomb.

Colonel Tibbets flew the Enola Gay on his historic mission to Hiroshima, Japan, on August 6, 1945.

DROPPING THE BOMB

At 2:45 a.m. on August 6, 1945, a B-29 bomber took off from the US Air Force base on Tinian Island in the South Pacific. The crew's mission was to fly approximately 1,500 miles (2,414 km) north to northwest across the Pacific Ocean to

Hiroshima, Japan. Upon arriving at approximately 8:00 a.m., they would drop an atomic bomb on the city.

In charge of the mission was Colonel Paul W. Tibbets, the commander of Group 509. The bomb "Little Boy," weighing 9,700 pounds (4,400 kg), was aboard his plane the *Enola Gay.* Few members of Tibbets's 12-man crew understood exactly what sort of weapon was on board, but they knew they were heading out on a top-secret mission to drop a bomb of enormous power.

Tibbets kept the *Enola Gay* at a low altitude for most of the flight but then climbed sharply to 31,000 feet (9,449 m) as the plane approached the target site. One minute before reaching the site, Tibbets told his crew to put on dark goggles to protect their eyes. Then at 8:15 a.m., they released the bomb.

Tibbets banked the plane sharply to turn away from the target and move out of the area as quickly as possible. Forty-three seconds later, the bomb burst 1,900 feet (579 m) over the city. Although the *Enola Gay* was already more than 11 miles (18 km) away from the target site, shock waves from the explosion rocked the plane. As the airmen looked back, they saw a giant mushroom-shaped cloud rise up over the city.

DETONATION

On the ground, the bomb's detonation caused an intense flash of light and a scorching wave of heat. Next came a tremendous blast with enough force to destroy nearly every building within an area of five square miles (13 sq km). The sky became black with dust and debris, hiding the sun from view. Fierce winds blew through the city, creating firestorms that eventually burned over four square miles (11 sq km). Within 20 to 30 minutes, heavy black rain that was full of soot and dust fell northwest of the city.

"[T]he enemy has begun to employ a new and most cruel bomb, the power of which to do damage is, indeed, incalculable, taking the toll of many innocent lives. Should we continue to fight, it would not only result in an ultimate collapse and obliteration of the Japanese nation . . . but would lead also to the total extinction of human civilization."[1]

—*Emperor Hirohito, in a radio address to Japan following the nation's surrender, August 15, 1945*

At the site of the blast, nine out of ten people are believed to have been killed instantly. Those near the blast who survived were severely burned by the scorching heat and blinded by the intense light. People further from the blast site were injured or killed when their homes, offices, and schools collapsed. Many more people were hurt or killed by fires and flying debris, such as shards of glass and splinters of wood. In all, approximately 70,000 people died from the initial effects of the blast.

Buildings were instantly destroyed and people killed when the atomic bomb was dropped on Hiroshima.

The Aftereffects

A few days after the bombing, survivors began showing signs of radiation sickness. The initial signs included nausea, vomiting, diarrhea, fever, and headaches. Later signs included loss of hair, bleeding from the nose and mouth, and a reduction of white blood cells, which left people at risk for infection. Many of these people died three to four weeks after the blast, but deaths from radiation poisoning continued for many more weeks. By the end of the year, 30,000 more people died, bringing the total to 100,000. And within five years, another 100,000 died. Additional

Facing
an Unknown Disease

In the book *Nagasaki 1945*, Dr. Tatsuichiro Akizuki wrote about radiation poisoning, then a puzzling new disease. Doctors reported observing symptoms that "suddenly appeared in certain patients with no apparent injuries."[3] Not until days after the blast did doctors realize they were observing the effects of radiation exposure. Akizuki wrote, "We were now able to label our unknown adversary 'atomic disease' or 'radioactive contamination' among other names. But they were only labels: we knew nothing about its cause or cure. . . . The disease destroyed [people] little by little. As a doctor, I was forced to face the slow and certain deaths of my patients."[4]

victims developed cancer, leukemia, and other fatal effects of radiation poisoning.

Americans learned about the bombing of Hiroshima late that morning, when radio stations broadcasted a prepared statement by President Truman. Truman warned that if Japan did not surrender immediately, additional targets would be bombed. Over the next few days, US planes dropped leaflets all over Japan that delivered this stern message: "We are in possession of the most destructive explosive ever devised by man. . . . We have just begun to use this weapon against your homeland."[2]

NAGASAKI

At approximately 11:00 a.m. on August 9, Major Charles Sweeney and his crew on a B-29 named *Bockscar* dropped "Fat Man" from the plane. At 11:02 a.m., the bomb exploded

1,650 feet (503 m) over the city of Nagasaki. The yield of this explosion was estimated at 40 percent greater than that of the Hiroshima bomb. Yet the damage was not as great, for several reasons.

The hills surrounding Nagasaki protected it somewhat from the immediate force of the blast, as well as the effects of the heat, fire, and radiation that followed. Also, the fact that the bomb was detonated over an industrial area meant that the residential and commercial areas of the city were less affected. And because of an air raid earlier in the month, some of the city's residents had been evacuated, including many schoolchildren.

Treating the Injured

After Hiroshima was bombed, providing medical treatment was nearly impossible. Many of the city's medical workers were either injured or dead and its hospitals and clinics were damaged.

In *Hiroshima,* a nonfiction book published in 1946, journalist John Hersey told the stories of several Japanese who survived the bombing. One was Dr. Sasaki, the only uninjured doctor at the Red Cross Hospital, the largest medical facility that received patients after the bombing. Hersey wrote:

After the explosion, [Dr. Sasaki] hurried to a storeroom to fetch bandages. This room, like everything he had seen as he ran through the hospital, was chaotic—bottles of medicines thrown off shelves and broken, salves spattered on the walls, instruments strewn everywhere. He grabbed up some bandages and an unbroken bottle of mercurochrome [antiseptic], hurried back to the chief surgeon, and bandaged his cuts. Then he went out into the corridor and began patching up the wounded patients and the doctors and nurses there.[5]

THE DAMAGE

Even so, the damage to Nagasaki was extensive. Nearly all buildings within one-half mile (0.8 km) of the targeted site were destroyed from the force of the blast, even those built to withstand earthquakes. And almost all homes within 1.5 miles (2.4 km) of the blast site were destroyed or damaged—approximately 20,000 in all. Nagasaki was not engulfed by firestorms, like Hiroshima was, but many fires broke out and caused additional damage.

The final death toll from the atomic bombing of Nagasaki is estimated at 140,000. Approximately 40,000 people are believed to have died instantly from the direct effects of the blast and another 60,000 injured. By year's end, another 30,000 people died, and within five years another 70,000 died.

The day after the bombing of Nagasaki, Emperor Hirohito overruled Japan's military leaders and surrendered. World War II was over.

Environmental Effects

The fact that the atomic bomb exploded above Hiroshima meant that most of its radioactive materials went up into the atmosphere, rather than down onto the ground. However, the rain that fell after the blast brought down some of these radioactive particles. They eventually washed into rivers, lakes, and other water sources, which eventually caused radiation poisoning in the people and animals that drank the contaminated water. This meant that some people who were not near the blast site still died from the effects of the bombing.

Survivors of the atomic bombings were exposed to high doses of radiation.

In 1949, Soviet nuclear tests made headlines in US newspapers.

The Nuclear Arms Race

Since the bombings of Japan, the development of nuclear weapons has continued at an increasing pace. By the end of 2010, nine countries were known to have the technology and materials needed to build a nuclear weapon.

THE COLD WAR

For a short time after World War II, the United States had the world's most powerful nuclear arsenal. US leaders used the nation's nuclear capability to keep the Soviet Union in check. Conflict between the two nations, which had emerged as the world's superpowers, was steadily increasing. This period was the start of the Cold War.

By the late 1950s, the Soviet Union had built an impressive nuclear arsenal of its own. Its newly developed nuclear missiles gave the Soviets the ability to strike targets in the United States and Western Europe from a distance. The frightening reality of this situation became clear in October 1962 during the Cuban Missile Crisis. At that time, US air surveillance photos showed Soviet missiles in Cuba— just 90 miles (144 km) off the Florida coast. The Soviets removed the missiles, but only after US forces created a blockade of Cuba and threatened additional military action. For 13 days during the crisis, though, the world was on the brink of nuclear war.

"The United States strongly seeks a lasting agreement for the discontinuance of nuclear weapons tests. We believe that this would be an important step toward reduction of international tensions and would open the way to further agreement on substantial measures of disarmament." [1]

—*President Dwight D. Eisenhower, letter to Soviet Premier Nikita Khrushchev, April 13, 1959*

By 1965, the Soviets had created a nuclear arsenal of some 6,300 weapons—up from only 200 in 1955. Ten years later, in 1975, the Soviet stockpile had grown to 17,900 weapons, and in 1985 it reached 29,000. The US arsenal was actually shrinking during this timeframe in response to worldwide efforts at nuclear arms control. Between 1965 and 1985, the United States reduced its nuclear arsenal from 32,400 to 23,500 weapons.

By 1985, the United States and the Soviet Union possessed a combined 52,500 nuclear weapons. That was enough power to destroy the entire world many times over. Ironically, having this mutual level of destructive ability put the two superpowers at a

The Cuban Missile Crisis

On October 15, 1962, a US surveillance plane discovered several Soviet nuclear missiles in Cuba. In the next few days, more missiles were discovered. When President John F. Kennedy confronted the Soviets, they denied having placed missiles in Cuba.

Kennedy responded with a naval blockade of Cuba and considered other military options, as well. Soviet ships waited in the waters off Cuba.

On October 26, after days of tense negotiations, the Soviet Union agreed to remove its missiles if the United States made a public statement promising not to invade Cuba. A day later, the Soviets also asked the United States to remove its own missiles from Turkey, located south of the Soviet Union. By Sunday, October 28, the crisis was considered over.

US warships remained just off Cuba for one more month until the Soviets removed the missiles and bombers capable of delivering nuclear weapons. In the spring of 1963, the United States removed its missiles from Turkey.

Some Soviet missiles left Cuba in November 1962, aboard the Soviet ship, the Divnogorsk.

stalemate. Neither of them could risk striking out against the other, because doing so would bring about the destruction of both.

The "Big Five"

The Cold War ended in 1991 with the collapse of the Soviet Union, but the threat of nuclear war was not over. After World War II, several other countries, along with the United States and the Soviet Union, began programs to develop nuclear weapons. Together they formed the "big five."

The United Kingdom launched their nuclear weapons program quite quickly. The British conducted their first successful atomic weapons test in October 1952.

In the mid-1950s, France began developing nuclear weapons. France detonated its first atomic bomb in February 1960.

China began developing nuclear weapons after the Korean War, because it viewed the United States as a serious military threat. From 1955 to 1958, the Chinese program depended on technological assistance from the Soviet Union. China detonated its first nuclear weapon in October 1964.

Soviet Spies

The Soviet nuclear weapons program was greatly assisted by the work of spies. This was first confirmed in 1950, when Klaus Fuchs and Julius and Ethel Rosenberg were arrested and executed for espionage. It was later revealed that spies had provided a huge amount of technical data to the Soviet weapons program, saving its scientists significant time and resources. In fact, the first plutonium bomb tested by the Soviets was a direct copy of the "Fat Man" bomb that was dropped on Nagasaki.

Ongoing Weapons Development

By the mid-1960s, the United States, the Soviet Union, the United Kingdom, France, and China were all recognized as nuclear states. In 1965, these five nations possessed a combined 39,047 nuclear weapons. That number increased to 52,323 in 1975 and to 68,585 in 1985 before dropping over the next several decades.

India began a nuclear weapons program in 1948, but did not test a nuclear device until 1974.

Immediately after the test, the Indian government announced a policy of not deploying nuclear weapons, despite having the technological ability. Then, on May 11, 1998, India reported that it had conducted a nuclear weapons test by detonating three nuclear devices at once, followed by two more devices just two days later.

Pakistan reportedly had the technology and materials to build a bomb by 1988. The Pakistani government announced that it had detonated six devices over a two-day period in May 1998.

Israel had built several nuclear devices by 1967. By the mid-1980s, Israel had an arsenal of 100 to 200 nuclear weapons, based on information obtained through espionage.

North Korea began developing nuclear weapons in the 1960s. In the early 1990s, US surveillance confirmed that the North Koreans had built several atomic weapons, but development stopped from 1994 to 2002 after the two nations reached an agreement. In October 2002, US surveillance discovered weapons activity once again. In 2006, North Korea announced it had tested a nuclear weapon. That test failed, but a more successful test occurred in 2009.

Iran is believed to have started a nuclear weapons program in the late 1970s. Work in the program was stalled between 1979 and 1988 by revolution and war, but it had resumed again by 1990—likely with assistance from Pakistan. In the early 2000s, survcillance located several facilities that seemed intended for nuclear weapons development. The Iranians insisted that the facilities were for developing nuclear power, not weapons. ⌐

Iran has one nuclear power plant at Bushehr.
It was recently loaded with uranium fuel.

The huge blast of a US nuclear weapons test could be seen above the Marshall Islands on July 25, 1946.

TYPES OF NUCLEAR WEAPONS

Nuclear weapons are the most powerful explosives ever developed. The blast they produce is so big that it is measured in kilotons (thousands of tons) and megatons (millions of tons) of TNT. The blast produces a tremendous shock wave, along with searing heat, blinding light, and lethal radiation. These deadly effects are all produced by a nuclear reaction: either fission or a combination of fission and fusion.

FISSION WEAPONS

The earliest nuclear weapons were created using a process called fission. It involves splitting heavier atoms to form lighter atoms. Fission weapons are sometimes called atomic bombs or A-bombs.

When fission occurs, the nucleus at the center of a heavy atom—such as uranium or plutonium—splits into several smaller particles and releases two or three neutrons. The neutrons that are released produce fission in at least one more nucleus, which splits and produces more neutrons. As this continues, it creates a chain reaction. With each instance of fission, energy is produced. During the complete chain reaction, a huge amount of energy is released within a few seconds.

The minimum quantity of fissionable material needed to sustain a chain reaction is called the

Testing Nuclear Bombs

The largest nuclear bombs built by the United States weighed up to 20 short tons (18 metric tons). But beginning in the early 1960s, the United States built a range of smaller, more lightweight weapons. By 1992—when live testing of nuclear weapons ended—the United States had conducted 1,030 tests of weapons of every imaginable size, shape, and purpose. After 1992, computers and other types of tests were used to verify weapons' safety and reliability.

critical mass. A quantity less than the critical amount is said to be subcritical, while a quantity greater than the critical amount is said to be supercritical. To produce a nuclear explosion, a subcritical mass of fissionable material must be brought rapidly to a supercritical level. At this point, the chain reaction begins and then continues until the energy produced is so great that the bomb blows itself apart.

The simplest type of fission weapon is the gun-assembly device. It works by firing one subcritical mass down a tube into another subcritical mass, thus creating a supercritical mass. Little Boy was this type of weapon.

The other major method of assembling a fission weapon is implosion. It works by compressing a subcritical mass of fissionable material into a dense critical mass through the use of a chemical explosive. Fat Man was this type of weapon.

Fusion Weapons

The process of fusion involves bonding lighter atoms to form heavier atoms. The nuclei of some forms of hydrogen and other light elements can be easily combined by subjecting them to extremely high temperatures—approximately tens of millions

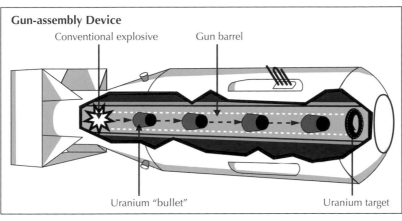

Gun-assembly Device

Conventional explosive   Gun barrel

Uranium "bullet"   Uranium target

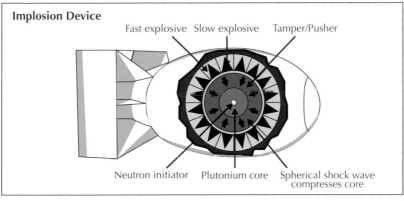

Implosion Device

Fast explosive   Slow explosive   Tamper/Pusher

Neutron initiator   Plutonium core   Spherical shock wave compresses core

There are two types of fission weapons:
the gun-assembly device and the implosion device.

of degrees. Doing so produces a heavier element and releases a large amount of energy.

Weapons produced using fusion are often called hydrogen bombs, H-bombs, or thermonuclear weapons. In this type of weapon, the required temperature and density of the materials are produced using a fission explosion. Fusion weapons typically release ten to 100 times as much energy as fission-only weapons.

A typical fusion bomb is constructed using a two-stage design. The first stage, called the primary, is a standard fission chain reaction. The radiation it produces heats the inside of the bomb to a temperature where a fusion reaction can be sustained. Under intense heat, the second stage of the bomb, called the secondary, completes the fusion reaction.

It is possible to construct a thermonuclear bomb with more than two stages. Both the Soviet Union and the United States produced three-stage weapons. In theory, the greater the number of stages, the greater the yield of the bomb. There is, however, a practical limit on how large and how heavy the bomb can become, because it somehow has to be delivered to the target site.

Developing the Hydrogen Bomb

In 1943, Oppenheimer invited Edward Teller to join the Manhattan Project, the goal of which was to develop an atomic bomb. Teller joined, but was more interested in developing a hydrogen bomb. In 1949, after the Soviet Union exploded an atomic bomb, Teller became determined that the United States had to develop the H-bomb— a more powerful weapon. President Truman agreed after learning that a spy had given the Soviets information from the US weapons program.

Delivery Systems

The first nuclear weapons, such as those used against Japan, were very heavy bombs that were delivered by airplane to the target site. For these early weapons, the lift capacity of an airplane determined how much the bombs could weigh. Also, the fact that these weapons had to fit inside an airplane meant that they had to be cylindrical in shape.

Beginning in the 1950s, design changes in nuclear weapons were related primarily to systems for delivering them. Miniaturization, or reducing the size of the weapons, was key. Improvements in both science and engineering allowed for

US versus Soviet Missile Development

During the Cold War, the development of cruise missiles and ballistic missiles was carried out primarily by the world's superpowers: the United States and the Soviet Union. And interestingly, these countries took very different approaches to developing missile technology.

For instance, the Soviets designed cruise missiles mainly for tactical use against ships at sea, not for strategic use against targets on land. Soviet submarines were fitted with cruise missiles to allow for so-called second-strike capability, or retaliation after being attacked. The United States followed the opposite approach, focusing their efforts on long-range, land-targeted missiles and put cruise missiles on bombers to attack targets far inside national boundaries and air defenses.

Also, in developing ballistic missiles, the United States concentrated on streamlining their weapons, producing greater accuracy but lower yields. In contrast, the Soviets built bigger missiles with higher yields, perhaps because they had difficulty solving guidance problems.

making much smaller, lighter weapons. The shape of the weapons changed, as well, from a cylinder to a sphere. These improvements provided greater flexibility in how nuclear weapons could be delivered and used.

By the 1960s, most heavy bombs had been replaced by strategic ballistic missiles. These rocket-type weapons were designed to deliver an explosive to a designated target at a great distance, with extreme accuracy, and at high speed. The explosive, called a warhead, was small enough to fit into the cone-shaped nose of the missile. The path of the weapon and the targeting of a specific site were controlled using a computer—then, a brand-new technology.

Soon, strategic ballistic missiles became the most important type of nuclear weapon, in large part because of the many delivery options they provided.

Ballistic versus Cruise Missiles

A ballistic missile is propelled into the air using a booster rocket. But once the missile has been launched, it is essentially a free-falling object whose path is affected by gravity and aerodynamics.

A cruise missile is self-powered, usually by some kind of jet engine. After being launched from an airplane, submarine, or land-based platform, it flies low to the ground to avoid detection by radar systems.

Nuclear-capable ballistic missiles can be launched
from the ground and do not need to be dropped from planes.

The shadow of a man and a ladder
were burned into a wall from the atomic blast at Nagasaki.

EFFECTS
OF NUCLEAR EXPLOSIONS

A nuclear explosion produces a wide
range of destructive effects, both
immediate and delayed. Within seconds or minutes
after detonation, near-total destruction over an
area between one and five miles (2 and 8 km) from

the point of detonation is caused by the blast and thermal radiation. And from a period of hours to days, months, and years, additional damage is caused by nuclear radiation and other environmental factors.

The Blast

When a nuclear weapon detonates, it produces a huge fireball. That fireball creates a shock wave of energy and pressure that grows larger with amazing speed—much like a tidal wave or tsunami. The front of the shock wave moves quickly away from the fireball, and its crushing pressure destroys almost everything in its path. Just ten seconds after detonation of a one-megaton (1 million metric tons) nuclear weapon, the front of the shock wave has traveled three miles (4.8 km). After 50 seconds, it has traveled approximately 12 miles (19.3 km) and is moving at a speed of 784 miles per hour (1,262 km/h).

A second destructive effect of the blast comes from the high-speed wind that follows the shock

Studying the Effects of Nuclear Explosions

The effects of nuclear explosions have been documented by data from several sources, including studies of the bombings of Hiroshima and Nagasaki, records kept from the more than 500 atmospheric tests and 1,500 underground tests conducted worldwide, and extensive calculations and computer models. Research has shown that the impact of a nuclear explosion depends on a range of factors: the design (fission or fusion) and yield of the weapon; whether the detonation occurs in the air, on the ground, underground, or underwater; the weather and other environmental conditions; and whether the target is an urban, rural, or military site.

wave. This wind can throw a standing person against a wall or building with a force several times the force of gravity. And because of this wind, the debris created by the blast—including bits of glass, wood, metal, and cement—flies through the air at speeds greater than 100 miles per hour (161 km/h), causing further damage.

Most injuries and deaths caused by the shock wave come from the collapse of buildings. People caught in their homes, schools, or offices can be crushed or suffocated. The impact that follows when a person is thrown in the air can also cause serious injury or death, as can being struck by flying debris. The high-speed wind that follows the shock wave also makes fires spread more quickly.

Firestorms

Under certain conditions, the many separate fires caused by a nuclear explosion can come together, forming a single, massive blaze called a firestorm. As the smaller fires blend, the air becomes extremely hot and directs hurricane-strength winds toward the fire, literally fanning the flames. The combination of the winds and the high temperature of the firestorm results in the burning of everything combustible near the blast site.

The firestorms in Hiroshima and Nagasaki were quite different because of both terrain and weather. The firestorm at Hiroshima burned 4.4 square miles (11.4 sq km), or approximately four times the area burned in Nagasaki. Hiroshima has a flat terrain, whereas Nagasaki is hilly and contained some water. In terms of weather, the conditions were clear the morning Hiroshima was bombed, but cloudy and rainy the morning Nagasaki was bombed.

THERMAL RADIATION

The fireball produced upon detonation of a nuclear weapon reaches approximately 180 million degrees Fahrenheit (100 million °C), which is comparable to the temperature at the center of the sun. Much of the energy produced by the nuclear weapon is released as light and heat, which is generally referred to as thermal energy or thermal radiation.

The fireball develops less than one-millionth of one second after the weapon's detonation. It immediately grows, expanding across and rising up into the air, like a balloon. Within seven-tenths of one millisecond, the fireball from a one-megaton weapon is approximately 440 feet (134 m) across. Within ten seconds, it has grown approximately 5,700 feet (1,737 m) across. At this point, the fireball is also rising at a speed of 250 to 350 feet per second (76 to 106 m/sec). Within one minute, it has risen approximately 4.5 miles (7.2 km) into the air.

The heat released by a nuclear explosion can cause dry materials—such as paper, dead leaves, and grass—to burst into flames. However, the primary cause of fires following a nuclear explosion is the shock wave produced by the blast. Buildings that

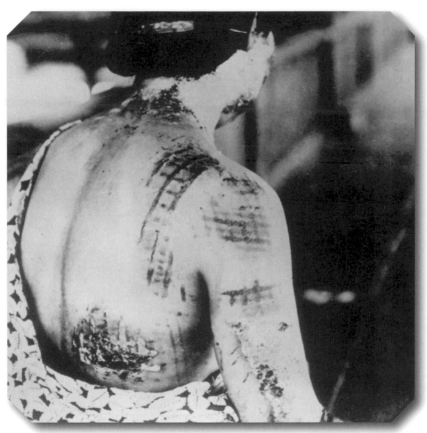

Radiation from the nuclear bombing of Hiroshima burned the pattern of a woman's kimono into her back.

have been damaged by the blast are likely to catch on fire for several reasons. In many cases, gas lines and fuel tanks have been broken or ruptured, spilling flammable mixtures. These mixtures are readily ignited by pilot lights, the gas flames in heating appliances such as stoves and furnaces.

BURNS AND BLINDNESS

People are affected by thermal radiation both directly and indirectly. Indirectly, they are victims of the fires that burn buildings after the blast. Directly, they are victims of flash burns, in which thermal energy sears their exposed skin. Flash burns are unique in that they affect only those areas of the skin facing the explosion. The most minor flash burns are like a bad sunburn, but more serious burns cause blistering and scarring and even the loss of skin tissue. Unless severe burns receive immediate and specialized treatment, the victim will likely die.

People are also vulnerable to the brilliant flash of light that follows a nuclear explosion. This form of thermal radiation causes flash blindness, which is a burn to the retina of the eye. Similar to a flash burn, flash blindness occurs only when the individual is looking directly at the blast. In most cases, the retinal damage is temporary, but under extreme conditions, permanent impairment can occur. Following a one-megaton explosion, flash blindness can occur from as far as 13 miles (21 km) away on a clear day and from as far as 53 miles (85 km) away on a clear night. Flash blindness is the most common type of injury following a nuclear explosion.

NUCLEAR RADIATION

Approximately 85 percent of the energy from a nuclear explosion produces air blast and thermal energy. The remaining 15 percent of the energy is released as nuclear radiation, which is toxic to human, animal, and plant life. Nuclear radiation is released both immediately—or within the first minute or so after the explosion—and over a longer period of time.

Initial radiation—the form released immediately— consists of radioactive rays and particles. The level of radiation is highest near the fireball, but because radioactive materials can penetrate most structures, the danger extends much further away. People close to the site of the explosion likely receive a lethal dose of nuclear radiation, but they are also hit by a deadly blast and surge of thermal energy, which kill them before the radiation has any effect. For this reason, relatively few deaths and injuries are caused by initial radiation.

Residual radiation—the second form of radiation—consists of radioactive particles that fall to the earth after a nuclear explosion. These particles, which are known as fallout, are bits of debris and by-products from the weapon and materials from the blast site, such as soil and water.

If the explosion occurs high above the ground, then the fallout will consist mainly of weapon debris and by-products, and most of these materials will rise into the atmosphere. If the explosion occurs on or near the ground, then soil, water, and other materials will also be sucked up into the rising cloud. These materials will become radioactive and contaminate the ground when they fall back down. Early fallout settles on the ground during the first 24 hours after the blast and has mostly local effects. Delayed fallout spreads across the earth during the following days and months and has worldwide effects.

SHORT- AND LONG-TERM EFFECTS

The effects of nuclear radiation on human beings depend mostly on the size of the dose. In the short term, low doses cause immediate hair loss, nausea, headaches, and loss of white blood cells. The loss of white blood cells creates a flu-like condition, which is referred to as mild radiation sickness. Higher

Hiroshima Survivors

The Hiroshima survivors, known as *hibakusha*, have shared many accounts of the bombing. Akihiro Takahashi, who was 14 at the time, said, "The heat was tremendous. And I felt like my body was burning all over. For my burning body the cold water of the river was as precious as the treasure. Then I left the river, and I walked . . . in the direction of my home. On the way, I ran into an another friend of mine. . . . I wondered why the soles of his feet were badly burnt. It was unthinkable to get burned there. But it was undeniable fact the soles were peeling and red muscle was exposed."[1]

doses of radiation can cause immediate damage to the thyroid, brain, and heart, even resulting in heart failure or death.

Over the long term, the effects of radiation poisoning include the development of cataracts, anemia and other blood disorders, and keloids (large, raised scars) on burned areas. More seriously, radiation sickness puts individuals at risk for various types of cancer, particularly leukemia and lymphoma, and makes them sterile, or unable to have children. Some of these long-term conditions do not develop for ten or more years following exposure to radiation.

OTHER ENVIRONMENTAL EFFECTS

Another effect of initial radiation is called the nuclear electromagnetic pulse (EMP). EMP can damage electronic equipment, including personal and business computers, telephones, and other devices along with high-level communication equipment and information systems. The damage from EMP is far-reaching, occurring up to thousands of miles from the blast site. The vulnerability of US military weapons and equipment to EMP was officially recognized in the 1960s, after electronic failures were observed following nuclear tests in several locations. Modern computer systems and microcircuits would be far more vulnerable to the effects of EMP.

Another environmental effect of nuclear explosions is depletion of the ozone layer of the atmosphere. The extreme heating and cooling of the air caused by a nuclear explosion produces nitric oxide, which destroys the ozone. The ozone layer protects the earth from harmful ultraviolet rays of the sun. Without it, significant climate and other ecological changes would occur.

A final environmental scenario is called the nuclear winter. Several well-respected scientists suggested this theory in 1983. They theorized that if a nuclear war occurred, the explosions would create firestorms and thus release huge amounts of smoke, soot, and dust into Earth's atmosphere. These materials could then block out most of the sun's light

Effects of EMP

Most people assume that if a nuclear weapon were detonated, it would target a specific site on the earth. However, given the effects of EMP, a weapon could be detonated high above Earth and knock out electronic equipment in the area below it. For example, if a high-yield weapon of approximately ten megatons (10 million metric tons) were detonated 200 miles (320 km) above the center of the United States, most of the country, along with parts of Mexico and Canada, would be affected by EMP. The effects would include damage or destruction of communications and electric power systems, resulting in economic and security issues.

for several weeks. The environmental conditions that could occur—semidarkness, below-freezing temperatures, and nuclear fallout—could destroy most of the planet's animal and plant life. Industry, communications, medicine, and transportation would also be affected. Ultimately, millions of people could die from starvation, disease, and exposure to the cold. In describing the theory of nuclear winter, the scientists concluded, "the possibility of the extinction of *Homo sapiens* cannot be excluded."[2]

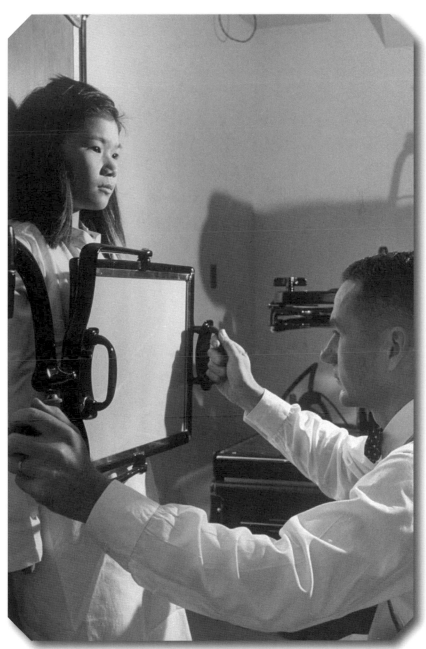

Doctors from the Atomic Bomb Casualty Commission
checked children for the effects of radiation sickness.

American physicists including Oppenheimer, far left, gave the United States a military advantage by being the first to design atomic weapons.

Nuclear Strategy

The concept of nuclear strategy involves establishing guidelines and plans for the development and use of nuclear weapons. In theory, nuclear strategy involves using military tools to achieve political goals. But throughout the nuclear weapons age, the primary goal has not been to wage and win a nuclear war. Rather, the primary goal has been to use nuclear weapons as a threat to deter attacks by others.

Unilateral Deterrence

The factors US leaders considered in deciding to bomb Japan in August 1945 demonstrate the first formation of nuclear strategy. US leaders wanted to use the atomic bomb to end World War II, and they believed that the surprise bombing of a mostly civilian target was necessary to bring about Japan's surrender. US leaders also considered to what extent their allies would be involved in making and carrying out these decisions. Although both the United Kingdom and the Soviet Union were US allies, the Soviets were left out of the discussion until just before the bomb was ready to be dropped.

Only four years later, in August 1949, the Soviets conducted their own nuclear weapons test. But for another ten years or so, the United States enjoyed a clear level of nuclear superiority. As the world's only nuclear power, the United States was able to set a policy of unilateral deterrence. The United States could threaten a nuclear strike without having to be concerned with another nation striking back. The term *massive retaliation* was used to describe the United States' planned response to a military attack, whether to itself or its allies.

At the same time, the United States took steps to maintain its military superiority. That meant developing weapons of different types and with greater power to build up the nation's nuclear arsenal. Doing so came at a tremendous financial cost.

MUTUAL DETERRENCE

In the mid-1950s, nuclear strategy became more complicated with the consideration of first- and second-strike capabilities. Strategists pointed out that if the United States were attacked first and unable to retaliate, the nation and its allies would be left vulnerable. These strategists recognized that having first-strike capability provided a clear advantage, in terms of national defense. But having the resources to survive a first strike and then retaliate

Civil Defense Training

In 1950, the US Congress created the Civil Defense Administration (CDA) with the intent of preparing the country for the out-break of nuclear war. CDA programs encouraged Americans to dig under-ground rooms in their backyards, called fallout shelters, and to stockpile nonperishable foods. In public schools, children were taught about nuclear radiation and survival techniques by a cartoon character called Bert the Turtle. After watching a cartoon called *Duck and Cover,* children practiced drills in which they hid underneath their desks in response to an air-raid siren.

with a second strike was also viewed as a significant element of nuclear strategy. In fact, second-strike capability provided a measure of stability, because it meant that no nuclear nation dared attack another.

The importance of second-strike capability was underscored by ongoing developments in nuclear weapons technology. Long-range bombers carrying nuclear weapons provided only limited second-strike capability, because they were vulnerable to being caught on the ground and to being shot down before reaching their targets. More

Sputnik

In 1957, Americans became worried about the possible superiority of Soviet technology following the launch of two satellites known as *Sputnik 1* and *Sputnik 2*. A third *Sputnik* was launched in 1958. The satellites had little military value, and the rocket that launched them was too primitive for use in launching missiles. Even so, Soviet Premier Nikita Khrushchev boasted that the country was turning out missiles "like sausages."[1]

Khrushchev's claim alarmed many Americans. They insisted that the United States outdo the Soviets in developing technology for both weapons and space exploration. To accomplish this goal, the US government was asked to provide more funding for education and to expand social programs that would improve the nation's image around the world. In addition, the government was asked to increase financial aid to undeveloped nations, which were viewed as vulnerable to Communist takeover.

President Eisenhower met the demands of concerned Americans. In 1958, he recommended the creation of the National Aeronautics and Space Administration (NASA) and passage of the National Defense Education Act. He also recommended acceleration of the US weapons programs.

The USS George Washington *was the Navy's first ballistic submarine.*

options for second-strike weapons and strategies came with the development of missiles in the early 1960s.

Intercontinental ballistic missiles (ICBMs) were hidden in sturdy underground silos, and submarine-launched ballistic missiles (SLBMs) were fitted on submarines. Neither type of missile was likely to be knocked out in a first-strike attack. These and other types of missiles also proved difficult to defend against, further increasing their deterrent value. Improved detection technologies, such as radar, were only effective for a short time.

The combination of long-range heavy bombers, ICBMs, and SLBMs served as the foundation of the United States' second-strike capability. Called the nuclear triad, it would continue to be a key piece of US nuclear weapons strategy into the twenty-first century.

By the mid-1960s, the Soviet Union and the United States had enough firepower to destroy one another, along with the rest of the world, many times over. The superpowers were locked into a situation known as mutual assured destruction (MAD). The nuclear standoff or stalemate that resulted was the basis for a policy of mutual deterrence.

ALTERNATIVES TO MAD

The MAD military strategy provided stability, since as long as both nations had the ability to destroy each other, no war would break out. The superpowers had every reason to maintain MAD because it gave them leverage as they began negotiating

Mutual Assured Destruction

Robert S. McNamara, US secretary of defense from 1961 to 1968, created the term *mutual assured destruction* (MAD). He argued that the relationship between the United States and the Soviet Union would be stable as long as each country was sure of the possibility of mutual assured destruction. In a 1967 speech, McNamara said, "No sane citizen, political leader or nation wants thermonuclear war. But merely not wanting it is not enough. We must understand the differences among actions which increase its risks, those which reduce them and those which, while costly, have little influence one way or another."[2]

arms control. Limiting the development and use of ballistic missiles was of special concern. But while many Americans hoped for arms reductions, strategists continued to explore alternatives to MAD.

One of those alternatives, called flexible response, involved the use of conventional military forces to avoid or delay the use of nuclear weapons. The United States had used the flexible-response approach in resolving the Cuban Missile Crisis in 1962, when the US Navy blockaded the Cuban harbor and prevented Soviet ships from entering. By the late 1960s, many world leaders considered conventional weapons useless and assumed that any future war would be a nuclear war. But as conflict escalated between the Soviets and the United States, the importance of stepping back from nuclear weapons became obvious.

In the 1970s, US nuclear strategy focused on conducting retaliatory strikes against selective targets—specifically, locations of Soviet leaders and military bases. The goal of this second-strike strategy, called countervailing, was to force the Soviet Union to surrender without destroying the entire nation. Ten years later, US strategists looked beyond merely countervailing and considered prevailing, or fighting and winning a limited nuclear war. Both defensive and offensive technologies were proposed, including an antimissile system that would put weapons in outer space.

Through it all, US and Soviet allies wondered what the superpowers' plans meant for their own national security. European nations, in particular, worried that the United States and the Soviet Union might fight a limited nuclear war on their continent.

Both US and Soviet strategists recognized that defending against a nuclear attack was virtually impossible, given the wide range and ongoing development of weapons delivery systems. Luckily, such an attack never happened. In December 1991, the collapse of the Soviet Union marked the end of the Cold War.

POST-COLD WAR STRATEGY

After the fall of the Soviet Union, the United States refocused its nuclear strategy yet again. Its immediate concern was Russia, the nation that had taken control of

The "Star Wars" System

In 1983, President Ronald Reagan proposed creation of an antimissile system called the Strategic Defense Initiative (SDI). The SDI was to be placed in outer space, allowing it to intercept Soviet missiles at various phases of flight. Plans included space- and ground-based laser battle stations and radar, optical, and infrared detection systems. Because of SDI's futuristic qualities, it was called "Star Wars" by its critics.

Work began on SDI, but the excessive technology and funding needed soon made the system impractical.

most of the Soviet arsenal. Hoping to encourage the Russians to dismantle much of that arsenal, the United States took some of its own weapons out of service. In 1991, a 20-year plan was put in place for both sides to continue reductions by an estimated 80 percent. The United States remained concerned, however, about the security of Russia's nuclear weapons and what would be done with the materials after the weapons were dismantled.

The United States also refocused on conventional war strategies. In fact, the US military had proven its power and readiness in January to February of 1991 during Operation Desert Storm, when it drove Iraqi forces out of Kuwait. The US Air Force was especially impressive in destroying Iraqi military targets and pinning down Iraqi troops. Technological advances in guidance and communication systems also helped the United States win a decisive victory.

Today, the use of a nuclear weapon—even an accidental use—seems increasingly likely, given the number and the nature of the countries that have nuclear weapons.

More conventional weaponry were used during Operation Desert Storm.

Find May Be Fossil of Nuclear Age

Piece of Steel

A large amount of steel was used in the construction of the weapon.

A remnant from an H-bomb accident is on display at the National Museum of Nuclear Science & History in Albuquerque, New Mexico.

ACCIDENTS AND INCIDENTS

The full details about accidents and incidents involving nuclear weapons will never be known. This kind of information is closely guarded by national governments, which are concerned with maintaining security and avoiding controversy.

The United States has released information at several times in the past 60 years. However, other governments—including those of the former Soviet Union and modern-day Russia—seldom release information.

DEFINITIONS OF TERMS

Reports about nuclear accidents often cover a range of mishaps and close calls. To clarify reporting, the US Department of Defense (DOD) has distinguished between an accident and an incident. The DOD has defined a *nuclear weapon accident* as an unexpected event involving nuclear weapons or nuclear weapons components that results in any of the following:

Accidental or unauthorized launching, firing, or use . . . which could create the risk of an outbreak of war;

Nuclear detonation, non-nuclear detonation or burning of a nuclear weapon or radioactive weapon component, . . .

Radioactive contamination;

Seizure, theft, or loss of a nuclear weapon component, including jettisoning [throwing off a ship];

Public hazard, actual or implied.[1]

To classify less serious mishaps, the DOD has defined a *nuclear weapon incident* as:

An unexpected event involving a nuclear weapon, facility, or component, resulting in any of the following, but not constituting a nuclear weapon accident:

[A]n increase in possibility of explosion or radioactive contamination;

[E]rrors committed in the assembly, testing, loading or transportation of equipment, and or the malfunctioning of equipment and material which could lead to an unintentional operation of all or part of the weapon arming and/or firing;

[A]ny act of God, unfavorable environment, or conditions resulting in damage to the weapon, facility or component. [2]

REPORTED ACCIDENTS AND INCIDENTS

The first nuclear weapon accident officially acknowledged by the US government occurred in February 1950, when a B-36 bomber dropped a nuclear bomb into the Pacific Ocean in fear that severe weather would cause the plane to crash. Between 1950 and 1968, 13 accidents occurred, based on a report released by the DOD. A 1980 report listed 32 accidents between 1950 and 1980, but did not include some accidents from the first report.

Neither DOD report identified an accident involving detonation of a nuclear weapon. However, a number of the accidents involved plane crashes in which explosions and fires caused the release of radioactive materials. Two of the worst accidents occurred in Palomares, Spain, in 1966, and in Thule, Greenland, in 1968. Each involved the crash of a B-52 bomber carrying four nuclear bombs. In the Palomares accident, the bomber collided with another plane in midair. The bombs fell to the ground and two exploded, releasing radioactive materials.

Critics have raised several concerns with the DOD reports. Clearly, the inconsistency in the number of accidents reported is of concern. Also, the reports include only those cases severe enough to be counted as nuclear weapon accidents. The number of incidents has apparently not been reported or

The "Two-Man Rule"

In addition to the security measures in place to guard nuclear weapons, other measures are in place to prevent an accidental or unauthorized detonation. One high-tech electronic system, called a permissive action link, requires entering two correct codes to arm a weapon. The codes are held by different people in different places and must be communicated following an order to arm the weapon. Following this "two-man rule" makes it almost impossible for one person to detonate a nuclear weapon alone if it is protected by this system. Not all nuclear weapons have this protection, though.

perhaps even documented. A final concern is that the DOD has not released another report since 1980.

Several environmental and humanitarian organizations have issued reports of nuclear weapon accidents and incidents, and their counts have tended to be higher than those from the DOD.

Nuclear Power Plants

Like a nuclear weapon, a nuclear power plant uses fission to create a large amount of energy. But in a power plant, the fission process is controlled so it does not reach the point of exploding. The energy created in a nuclear power plant heats water to create steam, which drives a turbine and generates electricity.

In 2007–2008, more than 439 nuclear power plants were in operation in 30 countries, providing approximately 14 percent of the world's electricity. France gets more of its electricity from nuclear power than any other nation, at 80 percent. The United States gets 20 percent of its electricity from 104 nuclear power plants.

Many Americans turned against the use of nuclear power after a near disaster occurred at the Three Mile Island plant near Harrisburg, Pennsylvania. In March 1979, over a period of several days, Americans watched and waited after an emergency was declared due to a mechanical failure. Approximately 140,000 people fled the area in a wave of panic. In the end, some radioactive materials were released into the air or water and officials confirmed that a nuclear accident had nearly occurred.

For example, in 1996, Greenpeace published a report listing 23 serious accidents involving US and Soviet weapons between 1950 and 1993. According to the report, 51 nuclear warheads were lost at sea (seven US warheads and 44 Soviet warheads). In addition, seven nuclear reactors were lost at sea during accidents involving nuclear-powered submarines (two US submarines and five Soviet submarines), and 19 reactors from other nuclear-powered vessels were deliberately dumped (one US vessel and 18 Soviet vessels).

Despite the lack of current reports, most sources agree that nuclear weapon accidents and incidents occurred more frequently during the Cold War for two reasons. First, in the early days of the nuclear era, the careful handling of weapons had not been perfected. Many accidents and incidents occurred along the way to developing security policies and procedures. And second, at the height of the arms race, there were close to 70,000 nuclear weapons on the planet. More weapons meant more mishaps of all kinds.

Today, there are considerably fewer weapons—approximately 30,000. An estimated 22,400

Nuclear Submarines

The world's first nuclear-powered submarine, the *USS Nautilus,* was launched by the US Navy in 1955. Fueled by a small nuclear reactor within a sealed compartment, this new sub could stay out at sea for extended periods of time. This quality made it an ideal tool for surveillance and other stealth operations.

By 1990, there were approximately 400 nuclear submarines at sea or in various stages of development. By 2000, approximately 300 of them had been decommissioned as the result of nuclear weapons reductions agreements. But a single US Trident ballistic missile submarine could destroy approximately 192 targets in any country on Earth, so even one of these is enormously powerful.

Walter Gregg and his family's home was destroyed in 1958 by an atomic bomb that was accidentally dropped by the US Air Force.

weapons are intact and 8,000 are operational. But a new problem has surfaced: how to safely store and keep track of the materials from dismantled weapons. These materials are still radioactive and they could be used to build new weapons.

TRAFFICKING AND TERRORISM

The large size of most nuclear weapons makes it unlikely they will be stolen. What is more likely is that the source materials used to initiate a nuclear reaction—particularly, uranium and plutonium—will be stolen. Plans for building weapons and other technological information are also common targets. Since the early 1990s, there have been many reports of these kinds of materials being stolen, sold, and smuggled by individuals and groups involved in worldwide trafficking.

The International Atomic and Energy Association (IAEA), whose purpose is to promote the safe use of nuclear technology, started recording trafficking incidents in 1993. By the end of 2001, the IAEA had recorded 181 confirmed incidents. Seventeen of them involved high-grade uranium or plutonium. Approximately half of these 17 incidents were recorded from 1993 to 1995—just several years after the collapse of the Soviet Union in 1991. Similar recordings by the US government identified 20 cases of trafficking of uranium and plutonium between May 1992 and July 2001, and in 15 of the cases the source of the materials was Russia, which had taken possession of many weapons in the Soviet arsenal.

Details of nuclear weapons trafficking became well known through reports about A. Q. Khan, the Pakistani engineer who once headed up his nation's nuclear weapons program. In 2004, the Pakistani government announced it had shut down a trafficking network run by Khan after discovering he had sold technological information to Libya. Khan was placed under house arrest and forbidden to leave Pakistan, but later reports indicated his network was still operating. It had sold information to Iran and North Korea, as well.

In 2004, plans for a small but powerful nuclear weapon were found on a laptop computer owned by individuals with direct ties to Khan. A UN agency weapons expert issued a report in 2008. He stated that given the electronic format of the plans, they could have been provided to multiple sources. In addition, the compact size of the weapon—which was small enough to be launched from a missile—would make it especially attractive to a rogue nation or terrorist group.

SECURITY MEASURES

In the United States, the primary responsibility for maintaining security of the country's nuclear weapons is shared by two federal agencies: the DOD and the National Nuclear Security Administration (NNSA), which is part of the Department of Energy. The DOD issues contracts for weapons and machinery and establishes US nuclear policy, strategy, and capabilities. The NNSA is primarily responsible for the management and security of US nuclear weapons, nuclear nonproliferation, and naval reactors. It also transports nuclear weapons to and from their initial military destinations and responds to nuclear emergencies.

Additional security is provided by the Domestic Nuclear Detection Office, an agency of the Department of Homeland Security. This agency is charged specifically with preventing nuclear weapons terrorism. Its activities have included developing radiation detectors that can be used at US airports, seaports, or other border crossings, improving security at the nation's nuclear laboratories, and tracking and shutting down networks of nuclear terrorists.

"The problem with such nuclear terrorism programs is that the threat is impossible to quantify. No one knows how much material may have been diverted to the black market—or who has purchased it there. Even worse, the targets could be anywhere and everywhere. What do you protect?"[3]

—*Nathan Hodge and Sharon Weinberger, in* A Nuclear Family Vacation: Travels in the World of Atomic Energy

The level of security that other nations provide for their nuclear weapons programs has been questioned and criticized, in some cases. The greatest concern is focused on Russia. Poorly kept records have made it impossible to know how many and what types of weapons Russia acquired from the former Soviet Union. This is particularly worrisome because of the size of the Soviet arsenal. Over approximately 45 years, the Soviet weapons program produced more than 1,000 short tons (893 metric tons) of radioactive materials. The loss of even 0.1 percent of these materials would provide enough to build dozens of new warheads.

To help address this issue, the United States has become involved in Russia's nuclear security. Since 1998, American scientists and security personnel have worked with their Russian counterparts to improve both safety and accountability. In 2011, Canada joined the United States in establishing a counterterrorism center in Abramovo, Russia. The center is to be used by Russia's defense ministry to train workers and improve security at the nation's nuclear sites.

President Barack Obama met with world leaders in 2010 at the Nuclear Security Summit to discuss the security of nuclear weapon materials.

The first international weapons agreement, signed in 1959, protected the pristine land of Antarctica.

NUCLEAR WEAPONS CONTROL

The first step toward nuclear weapons control was taken in 1957, with the establishment of the International Atomic Energy Agency (IAEA). Sponsored by the United Nations (UN), the IAEA is an independent organization made up of representatives of various countries. The agency's purposes are to promote peaceful uses of nuclear technology and to prevent military purposes of that technology. Even today, the IAEA has primary oversight of the world's nuclear technology.

The first international agreement aimed at controlling nuclear weapons was the Antarctic Treaty of 1959. Signed by the United States, the Soviet Union, and ten other countries, this agreement declared Antarctica an international, military-free region and prohibited the conducting of nuclear weapons tests or disposing of nuclear waste there.

In the 1960s, the United States, the Soviet Union, and the United Kingdom made several agreements that were of limited risk to each nation. For example, the Nuclear Test Ban Treaty, signed in 1963, restricted the testing of

The International Atomic Energy Agency

Critics of the IAEA have stated that the agency has the authority to conduct inspections and report results but no power to enforce rules or penalize violators. The IAEA's effectiveness is further limited by the fact that it can only inspect the nuclear facilities of nations that are part of the NPT and allow it access. Likewise, the IAEA lacks the power to investigate nuclear weapons trafficking or cheating by NPT countries that have pledged to remain nonnuclear. For the IAEA to take on these responsibilities, the NPT would have to be substantially revised.

nuclear weapons to underground sites by prohibiting testing in the atmosphere, in outer space, and under water. In 1967, the Outer Space Treaty went a step further by prohibiting the placement of nuclear weapons and other weapons of mass destruction in Earth's orbit.

NUCLEAR NONPROLIFERATION TREATY

By the mid-1960s, five nations had nuclear weapons: the United States, the Soviet Union, the United Kingdom, France, and China. These nations were recognized as nuclear states in 1968 with the drafting of the Nuclear Nonproliferation Treaty (NPT). With that recognition came the pledge not to support the proliferation of nuclear weapons to countries that did not already have them. Those countries, called nonnuclear states, pledged not to acquire nuclear weapons or the

The "Hot Line"

In the early days of the Cold War, negotiators learned the importance of maintaining clear, direct communication between the US and Soviet leaders. In 1962, much of the negotiation during the Cuban Missile Crisis was conducted using written documents, which took time to travel and be decoded, exchanged between the nations' leaders. To allow for faster communication and to reduce the risk of misunderstanding in the case of an accident, a direct phone line—called the "hot line"—was established in 1963 between Washington DC and Moscow, the Soviet capital.

technology needed to make them. All countries agreed to allow the IAEA to inspect their nuclear power and weapons facilities.

The NPT took effect in 1970 and by 1995 was signed by 62 countries. In 1995, the initial 25-year term of the treaty was extended indefinitely, and by 2005, 187 nations had joined.

STRATEGIC ARMS LIMITATION TALKS

During the 1970s, the superpowers participated in the Strategic Arms Limitation Talks (SALT). The first two agreements—SALT I and SALT II—were signed by the United States and the Soviet Union in 1972 and 1979, respectively.

SALT I was the product of three years of negotiations and included a complex set of agreements. One of the key agreements was the Anti-Ballistic Missile (ABM) Treaty of 1972, which regulated weapons that could be used to destroy incoming ICBMs. Restricting the number of these weapons prevented both the Soviet Union and the United States from being able to defend large areas of their countries, thus preserving mutual deterrence. Another key piece of SALT I was the Interim Agreement and Protocol on Limitation of

The SALT II treaty was signed by Soviet president Leonid Brezhnev and US president Jimmy Carter on June 19, 1979.

Strategic Offensive Weapons, which froze existing levels of ICBMs and SLBMs.

Negotiations for SALT II began in 1972, after the signing of the previous agreement, and continued for seven years. Reaching agreement proved difficult because the Soviet Union and the United States had followed different priorities in building their arsenals, which raised questions about which types of weapons technology should be limited. Ultimately, SALT II set limits on long-range bombers and strategic launchers.

Overall, the SALT agreements were successful in slowing down the nuclear arms race between the Soviet Union and the United States. However, the weapons levels that were set were quite high, leaving each superpower with more than enough firepower to destroy the other dozens of times over.

STRATEGIC ARMS REDUCTION TALKS

Beginning in 1982, negotiations between the superpowers took a new direction by focusing on reducing numbers of existing warheads and means of delivering them. Called the Strategic Arms Reduction Talks (START), these negotiations would continue into the 2000s and produce another series of agreements.

The START I agreement, reached in July 1991, committed the United States and the Soviet Union to reduce numbers of strategic nuclear weapons by 15 to 30 percent over several years. The two nations also agreed to reduce certain types of existing tactical nuclear weapons, or those designed for use by forces on the battlefield. This START agreement extended the 1990 Conventional Forces in Europe Treaty, which had committed most Soviet and US allies to similar arms reductions.

In December 1991, the Soviet Union broke up, and several newly independent republics took over weapons from the Soviets' nuclear stockpile. Ukraine, Belarus, and Kazakhstan quickly moved toward complete nuclear disarmament, and all three had accomplished that by 1996. Russia acted both on its own and in agreement with the United States to make sizeable reductions to its arsenal of nuclear and conventional weapons. In 1993, the two nations agreed to terms in START II, which called for reducing strategic nuclear forces over a timeframe extending into the 2000s.

In 1996, negotiations among world leaders produced the Comprehensive Test Ban Treaty, which prohibited the testing of all nuclear weapons in the air, under the water, and below the ground. The treaty was signed by 182 countries, but it was prevented from taking effect. Several key countries had decided not to sign or ratify the treaty—among them, China, India, Israel, North Korea, Pakistan, and the United States, which are all nuclear weapons powers.

In January 2002, the United States ignored international opposition and withdrew from the ABM Treaty—the first time the nation had withdrawn from a treaty in the nuclear age. Even though Russia was not happy with this decision, it joined the United States in May in signing the Strategic Offensive Reductions Treaty. Russia also announced that it was withdrawing from START II.

In December 2009, START I expired with no other agreement in place. After starting new negotiations, Russia and the United States agreed to terms in April 2010, signing the New Strategic Arms Reduction Treaty. That agreement, called New START, allowed each country to deploy only 1,550 strategic nuclear warheads—down from 6,000 in START I and down from tens of thousands of strategic warheads during the Cold War—and also called for reductions in other nuclear and conventional weapons. The agreement also established a new system for inspecting and monitoring nuclear facilities and engaged other nations in securing the world's nuclear materials.

A Proven Success

One of the most successful examples of nuclear weapons control was the Intermediate-Range Nuclear Forces Treaty (INF), which was in effect from 1988 to 2000. Under this agreement, the Soviet Union and the United States eliminated an entire class of nuclear missiles. In addition, the INF opened up communication in weapons control by providing for short-notice inspections and constant monitoring of weapons assembly plants. During the 13 years of the INF, 851 inspections were conducted: 540 by the United States and 311 by the Soviet Union and its successors.

CURRENT CHALLENGES

Although the NPT has been applauded for setting
standards for world disarmament, critics have judged
it as unfair and unrealistic. In accordance with the
NPT's original terms, only the "big five" continue
to be recognized as nuclear states, despite the fact
that by 2010, at least four more countries were
known to have nuclear weapons capabilities: India,
Israel, North Korea, and Pakistan. Three of these
countries are among only four worldwide that have
not signed the NPT (Cuba is the fourth). India and
Pakistan have suffered no severe penalties from the
international community for failing to sign, and
India and Israel are closely allied with the United
States.

It is a very real possibility that nuclear weapons
traffickers will provide an unstable nation or
terrorist group with the materials or technology
needed to build a weapon. The key factors in this
scenario are Russia's lax security in tracking nuclear
weapons and radioactive materials and proof that
North Korea, Iran, and Libya have all obtained
weapons materials and technology from traffickers.

Today, the "big five" have a combined nuclear
arsenal of approximately 30,000 weapons—which is

a reduction of more than half since 1985. But this reduction by the world's leaders has been offset by the development of nuclear weapons by some of the world's most unstable countries. North Korea and Pakistan are considered likely to engage in war. And they are located in the Middle East or Asia, as are India and Israel, which tend to be politically volatile regions of the world. Nuclear weapons strategists today fear that this combination of factors could set the stage for another world war—perhaps

Effects of Nuclear Weapons Testing

Beginning with the Trinity Test in July 1945, the number of aboveground nuclear tests increased steadily from year to year. From 1949 to 1961, there were 141 atmospheric tests. By 1963, 545 nuclear weapons had been detonated in atmospheric tests.

In addition to increasing in number, the tests also grew in yield. From 1945 to 1951, the energy released into the atmosphere by nuclear testing was estimated at 600 kilotons. From 1951 to 1962, the amount of energy released had increased by 1,000 times.

Nuclear weapons tests were conducted in isolated areas to protect people from exposure to radioactive materials. But the tests released massive amounts of materials into the atmosphere, exposing people worldwide to a low but steady dose of radiation in the form of fallout. And in areas where extensive testing was conducted, including islands in the South Pacific, the level of radiation is so high that the areas are uninhabitable. A final product of nuclear testing is the large amount of radioactive waste produced. One estimate has put the cost of cleaning up US nuclear weapons facilities at $1 trillion.

In 1963, the Nuclear Test Ban Treaty forced testing to go underground. Underground testing is believed to have few immediate environmental effects.

a nuclear world war. In the future, more work and more cooperation in the world community will be needed to prevent such an unthinkable disaster from occurring. ⟶

South Koreans protested after North Korea conducted a nuclear test in 2009.

TIMELINE

1938	1941	1945
German scientist Otto Hahn successfully splits the atom.	In December, the project to build an atomic bomb, code-named the Manhattan Project, is launched.	On July 16, the United States conducts the world's first atomic bomb test, called the Trinity Test.

Mid-1950s	1957
Nuclear strategy becomes more advanced with the consideration of first- and second-strike capabilities.	The International Atomic Energy Agency is established to promote peaceful uses of nuclear technology.

1945

On August 6 and 9, the United States drops atomic bombs on Hiroshima and Nagasaki, Japan, respectively.

1949

The Soviet Union conducts its first nuclear weapons test.

1950

In February, the US government officially acknowledges the first nuclear weapon accident.

1959

The Antarctic Treaty, the first international agreement aimed at controlling nuclear weapons, establishes Antarctica as a nuclear-free zone.

1960s

Strategic missiles become the most important type of nuclear weaponry and provide more second-strike options.

1962

From October 15 to 28, the world is on the brink of nuclear war during the Cuban Missile Crisis.

TIMELINE

1963	1970	1972
The Nuclear Test Ban Treaty prohibits testing nuclear weapons in the atmosphere, under water, and in outer space.	The Nuclear Nonproliferation Treaty goes into effect, recognizing five nuclear states.	SALT I places restrictions on levels of US and Soviet ballistic missiles.

1991	1993	1996
In December, the Soviet Union collapses, ending the Cold War.	In January, START II calls for Russia to reduce strategic nuclear forces over a timeframe extending into the 2000s.	Negotiations lead to the Comprehensive Test Ban Treaty but it is prevented from taking effect.

1979

SALT II sets limits
on US and Soviet
long-range bombers
and strategic
launchers.

1985

The "big five"
have a combined
nuclear arsenal
of 68,585 weapons
—the largest amount
ever accumulated.

1991

In July,
START I commits
the United States and
the Soviet Union to
reduce levels of both
strategic and tactical
nuclear weapons.

2002

The United States
withdraws from
the ABM Treaty,
and Russia withdraws
from START II.

2004

The Pakistani
government admits
that A. Q. Khan
has been operating
a weapons trafficking
network.

2010

In April,
the United States
and Russia sign
New START.

Essential Facts

At Issue

❖ The United States developed and deployed the world's first nuclear bombs to force Japan to surrender and thus end World War II.

❖ During the Cold War, the United States and the Soviet Union reached a stalemate after recognizing their ability for mutual assured destruction (MAD).

❖ The nuclear arms race reached its peak in 1985, when the US and Soviet Union had enough nuclear weapons to destroy the world dozens of times over.

❖ The blast from a nuclear explosion produces a tremendous shock wave, along with an often deadly level of thermal radiation. Nuclear radiation causes severe burns and puts people at long-term risk for cancer. Radiation released into the atmosphere returns to the earth as fallout and contaminates the land and water.

❖ The development of missile technology in the 1960s provided multiple options for delivering nuclear warheads and thus changed nuclear strategy to focus on responding to an attack, called second-strike capability.

❖ Efforts at nuclear weapons control have focused on disarmament, or reducing types and numbers of weapons; on limiting the development, testing, and deployment of weapons; and on using negotiation to settle conflicts peacefully and to encourage participation in international organizations and agreements that represent mutual interests.

❖ The reduction of nuclear weapons among the world's leaders has been offset by the development of weapons by some of the world's most unstable countries.

Critical Dates

1941
In December, the project to build an atomic bomb, code-named the Manhattan Project, was launched.

1945

On August 6 and 9, atomic bombs were dropped on Hiroshima and Nagasaki, Japan, respectively.

1962

From October 15 to 28, the world was on the brink of nuclear war during the Cuban Missile Crisis.

1963

The Nuclear Test Ban Treaty prohibited testing nuclear weapons in the atmosphere, under water, and in outer space.

1970

The Nuclear Nonproliferation Treaty (NPT) established the "big five" as nuclear states and all other countries as nonnuclear states.

1991

In December, the Soviet Union collapsed, ending the Cold War.

Quotes

"[T]he enemy has begun to employ a new and most cruel bomb, the power of which to do damage is, indeed, incalculable, taking the toll of many innocent lives. Should we continue to fight, it would not only result in an ultimate collapse and obliteration of the Japanese nation . . . but would lead also to the total extinction of human civilization."—*Emperor Hirohito, August 15, 1945*

"The problem with such nuclear terrorism programs is that the threat is impossible to quantify. No one knows how much material may have been diverted to the black market—or who has purchased it there. Even worse, the targets could be anywhere and everywhere. What do you protect?"—*Nathan Hodge and Sharon Weinberger, in* A Nuclear Family Vacation: Travels in the World of Atomic Energy

GLOSSARY

arsenal
    A storehouse or stockpile of weapons.

deploy
    To install or make ready for use.

deterrence
    Avoidance or prevention.

detonated
    Exploded.

disarmament
    The reduction of weapons.

fallout
    Radioactive particles that fall back to the earth after a nuclear explosion.

fission
    The splitting of heavier atoms to form lighter atoms.

fusion
    The bonding of lighter atoms to form heavier atoms.

monitor
    To check or review on a regular basis.

nuclear radiation
    Particles released from the nucleus of an atom as the result of nuclear fission.

proliferation
    The act of increasing or spreading.

rogue
    Unpredictable and independent.

strategic weapons
> Nuclear weapons that can travel a long distance and that carry a large, powerful warhead; these weapons are designed to be used against a predetermined target, such as a military base, as part of a war plan.

surveillance
> Close observation, especially of a suspicious person or group.

tactical weapons
> Nuclear weapons that can travel a short distance and that carry a smaller, less powerful warhead; designed to be used in the battlefield on an as-needed basis.

thermal radiation
> The intense heat and light produced by a nuclear explosion.

trafficking
> The illegal or unethical selling and transporting of a product, such as weapons or drugs.

unilateral
> One way or one-sided.

warhead
> The tip of a nuclear missile, which carries the explosive device.

yield
> The amount of energy released when a nuclear weapon explodes; usually expressed in kilotons (thousands of tons) or megatons (millions of tons) of TNT.

ADDITIONAL RESOURCES

SELECTED BIBLIOGRAPHY

Hersey, John. *Hiroshima.* New York: Vintage, 1946. Print.

Hodge, Nathan, and Sharon Weinberger. *A Nuclear Family Vacation: Travels in the World of Atomic Energy.* New York: Bloomsbury, 2008. Print.

Reed, Thomas C., and Danny B. Stillman. *The Nuclear Express: A Political History of the Bomb and Its Proliferation.* Minneapolis, MN: Zenith, 2009. Print.

Takaki, Ronald. *Hiroshima: Why America Dropped the Atomic Bomb.* Boston: Little, 1993. Print.

FURTHER READINGS

Friedman, Lauri S. *Nuclear Weapons and Security*. San Diego, CA: ReferencePoint, 2008. Print.

Henningfeld, Diane Andrews, ed. *Weapons of War*. Detroit: Greenhaven, 2011. Print.

Miller, Debra A. ed. *Nuclear Armament*. Detroit: Greenhaven, 2011. Print.

Sheen, Barbara. *Nuclear Weapons*. Yankton, SD: Erickson, 2007. Print.

WEB LINKS

To learn more about nuclear weapons, visit ABDO Publishing Company online at **www.abdopublishing.com**. Web sites about nuclear weapons are featured on our Book Links page. These links are routinely monitored and updated to provide the most current information available.

For More Information

For more information on this subject, contact or visit the following organizations.

Bradbury Science Museum
1350 Central Avenue
Los Alamos, NM 87544
505-667-4444
http://www.lanl.gov/museum
Operated by the Los Alamos National Laboratory, this museum features three galleries: a History Gallery with artifacts and information about development of the atomic bomb; a Defense Gallery that examines the defense mission of the laboratory; and a Research Gallery that reviews the scientific work at Los Alamos.

Hiroshima Peace Memorial Museum
1–2 Nakajimama-cho
Naka-ku, Hiroshima City 730-0811, Japan
011-81-82-242-7798
http://www.pcf.city.hiroshima.jp/index_e2.html
This museum provides information about life in Japan before and after the war, the atomic bomb and nuclear weapons development, and the preservation of peace worldwide. Special features include a virtual tour, a printable museum pamphlet (available in ten languages), and a Kids Peace Station.

The National Museum of Nuclear Science & History
601 Eubank Blvd. SE
Albuquerque, NM 87123
505-245-2137
http://www.nuclearmuseum.org
This museum tells the story of the atomic age—from the days of early research and development through the current era of peaceful uses of nuclear technology.

SOURCE NOTES

Chapter 1. Global Tensions in the Nuclear Age

1. "North Korean Attack Comes Amid Regime Succession, as Obama Calls Act 'Provocative.'" *FoxNews.com*. Fox News, 23 Nov. 2010. Web. 1 Feb. 2011.

2. William J. Broad and David E. Sanger. "The Bomb Merchant: Chasing Dr. Khan's Network; As Nuclear Secrets Emerge, More Are Suspected" *NYTimes.com*. New York Times, 26 Dec. 2010. Web. 3 Mar. 2011.

Chapter 2. Building the Bomb

1. "Einstein's Letter to President Roosevelt—1939." Library: Historical Documents: The Atomic Age Begins. *Atomicarchive.com*. Atomic Archive, n.d. Web. 1 Feb. 2011.

2. Gideon Rose. *How Wars End: Why We Always Fight the Last Battle*. New York: Simon, 2010. Print. 114.

3. Daniel Patrick Moynihan. *Secrecy: The American Experience*. New Haven, CT: Yale UP, 1999. Print. 136.

4. "Potsdam Declaration." Library: Historical Documents: The Bombing of Hiroshima and Nagasaki. *Atomicarchive.com*. Atomic Archive, n.d. Web. 1 Feb. 2011.

Chapter 3. Dropping the Bomb

1. "Emperor Hirohito, Accepting the Potsdam Declaration, Radio Broadcast." Documents Relating to American Foreign Policy: Hiroshima. *Mtholyhoke.edu*. Mount Holyoke College, n.d. Web. 1 Feb. 2011.

2. "Leaflets Dropped On Cities In Japan." *PBS.org*. PBS, n.d. Web. 3 Mar. 2011.

3. "Radiation Effects on Humans." *Thinkquest.org*. Oracle ThinkQuest, Education Foundation, n.d. Web. 1 Feb. 2011.

4. Ibid.

5. "John Hersey." Second World War. *Spartacus.schoolnet*. Spartacus Educational, n.d. Web. 1 Feb. 2011.

Chapter 4. The Nuclear Arms Race
    1. "Selected Nuclear Quotations." *cdi.org*. Center for Defense Information, n.d. Web. 2 Mar. 2011.

Chapter 5. Types of Nuclear Weapons
None.

Chapter 6. Effects of Nuclear Explosions
    1. "The Story of Hiroshima: Hibakusha Stories." History: Tale of Two Cities: Hiroshima and Nagasaki. *Atomicarchive.com*. Atomic Archive, n.d. Web. 1 Feb. 2011.
    2. Gynne Dyer. *War: The Lethal Custom*. New York: Carroll and Graf, 2004. Print. 344.

Chapter 7. Nuclear Strategy
    1. Walter A. McDougall, primary contributor. "The World After Sputnik: Soviet Progress and American Reaction." *Britannica.com*. Encyclopedia Britannica Online, 2011. Web. 1 Feb. 2011.
    2. Robert S. McNamara. "'Mutual Deterrence' Speech by Sec. of Defense Robert McNamara." Library: Historical Documents: Arms Control, Deterrence and Nuclear Proliferation. *Atomicarchive.com*. Atomic Archive, n.d. Web. 1 Feb. 2011.

Source Notes Continued

Chapter 8. Accidents and Incidents

1. Jaya Tiwari and Cleve J. Gray. "U.S. Nuclear Weapons Accidents." *CDI.org.* Center for Defense Information, n.d. Web. 1 Feb. 2011.

2. Ibid.

3. Nathan Hodge and Sharon Weinberger. *A Nuclear Family Vacation: Travels in the World of Atomic Energy.* New York: Bloomsbury, 2008. Print. 65–66.

Chapter 9. Nuclear Weapons Control

None.

Index

INDEX CONTINUED

ABOUT THE AUTHOR

Susan M. Freese, a freelance writer and editor, holds BA and MA degrees in English. During her career, she has developed and produced educational materials for students of many levels. She has also taught college-level literature, writing, and communication courses. Susan's interest in music and the arts has involved her in writing promotional and grant materials for several nonprofit organizations, including the Medalist Fine Arts Association and the Bloomington Fine Arts Council. She is also the current president of the Minnesota Bookbuilders, a group of professionals who work in various facets of producing books. Susan lives in Minneapolis, Minnesota.

PHOTO CREDITS

AP Images, cover, 3, 6, 15, 23, 26, 29, 37, 42, 49, 54, 88, 97 (top), 97 (bottom), 99 (top), 99 (bottom left); Kyodo/AP Images, 10; Keystone-France/Gamma-Keystone/Getty Images, 16; PhotoQuest/Getty Images, 25, 96; Alfred Eisenstaedt/Time & Life Pictures/Getty Images, 33; Keystone/Getty Images, 34; Vahid Salemi/AP Images, 41; Red Line Editorial, 45; Authenticated News/Getty Images, 50; Carl Mydans/Time & Life Pictures/Getty Images, 61; Hulton Archive/Getty Images, 62; Frank Curtin/AP Images, 66; Jordan/AP Images, 71; Michael J. Gallegos/AP Images, 72; Don Cravens/Time & Life Pictures/Getty Images, 78; Jewel Samad/AFP/Getty Images, 83, 99 (bottom right); Ryan T. Pierse/Getty Images, 84; Chung Sung-Jun/Getty Images, 95